Who Will
Prince H

GW01464188

Tony Bradman

Illustrated by Aleksei Bitskoff

For our son Tom –
another young man who's having far too much fun

T.B.

To my son Tim –
our Commander-in-Chief in little pants!

A.B.

EGMONT
We bring stories to life

Book Band: Gold
First published in Great Britain 2016
by Egmont UK Limited
The Yellow Building, 1 Nicholas Road, London, W11 4AN
Text copyright © Tony Bradman 2016
Illustrations copyright © Aleksei Bitskoff 2016
The author and illustrator have asserted their moral rights.
ISBN 9 780 6035 7351 4
A CIP catalogue record for this title is available from the British Library.
Printed in Malaysia.
67754/1

All rights reserved. No part of this publication may be reproduced, stored in a retrieval system, or transmitted, in any form or by any means, electronic, mechanical, photocopying, recording or otherwise, without the prior permission of the publisher and copyright owner.
Stay safe online. Egmont is not responsible for content hosted by third parties.

Series and book banding consultant: Nikki Gamble

Contents

Reading Ladder

Too Much Fun

Prince Harry woke up and jumped out of bed with a big smile.

The sun was shining in a cloudless blue sky, birds were twittering in the woods, and the delicious smell of a tasty breakfast was wafting its way to him from downstairs.

Harry quickly got dressed, then he went through the list of activities he had planned for the day. Harry *loved* making lists, and this one was full of his favourite things. The day was going to be packed, but that was the way he liked it . . .

1. Breakfast.
2. Riding.
3. Play on computer.
4. Read new book.
5. Lunch.
6. More playing on computer.
7. More reading.
8. More riding.
9. Dinner.
10. Watch TV.
11. Make list for next day.
12. Bed.
13. More reading.
14. Midnight snack.
15. Sleep.

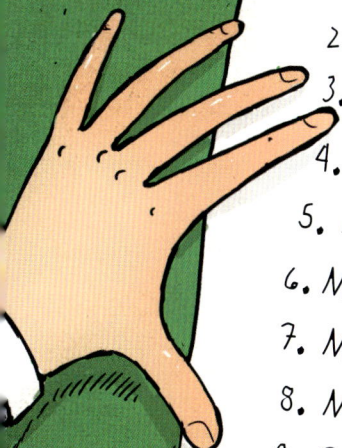

He skipped downstairs whistling a merry tune. His parents, the king and queen, were sitting at the long table in the dining hall.

'Good morning, Mother and Father!' said Harry. 'I trust you're both feeling cheerful today?'

'No, Harry, we're not,' said the king. 'In fact we're very unhappy.'

'Oh dear,' murmured Harry, not taking much notice. He was too busy piling food on to his plate. Besides, his parents had been very grumpy lately.

'I'm sorry to hear that,' he added. 'Is there anything I can do to help?'

'There is, as it happens,' said the queen. 'You can get married.'

'Excuse me?' spluttered Harry. He nearly choked on a piece of toast, but then he laughed. 'Oh, very funny, Mother. You and your jokes . . . I almost fell for that one!'

'Your mother isn't joking, Harry.' The king raised an eyebrow. 'We're deadly serious.'

'But I don't want to get married,' said Harry. 'I'm having too much fun.'

'Exactly,' said the queen. 'All you do is enjoy yourself, and it's got to stop. You need to get ready to run the country. We won't be around forever, you know.'

'You're not ill, are you?' said Harry, suddenly worried about them.

'We're fine,' said the king. 'But we'd like to retire. You've had your fun, and now it's time for us to have ours. I've always wanted to go on a cruise . . .'

11

'That's fair enough, I suppose,' said Harry. 'But why do I have to get married?'

'Running the country is a job for two people,' said the queen. 'It's hard work.'

Harry sighed. He didn't like the sound of that at all.

Stylists and Hairdressers

After breakfast, Harry tried to sneak off, but he didn't get very far.

'Where are you going, Harry?' said the king. 'Come back this instant!'

'But I've got a lot planned for today,' said Harry. 'Look, here's my list.'

'Well, you can forget all that,' said the queen.

She crossed out everything that was on Harry's list and added one new task. 'We've got to make a start on finding you a wife.'

It turned out that they had already signed up to some websites – RoyalMatch.com, PrincessBride.com and FairyTalePartner.com. So Harry spent the rest of the morning scrolling through the profiles of dozens of princesses.

'What about her?' said the queen. 'She sounds great! This one does too . . .'

Harry wasn't sure about any of them, but he tried to stay positive. He felt a lot better once he'd made a list of princesses he wouldn't mind meeting. There was a longer list of princesses he never wanted to meet, but he kept that to himself.

'Terrific!' said the king, slapping him on the back. 'We'll set up some dates.'

The next day the princesses jetted in
from all over the world. They brought gaggles
of stylists and hairdressers and friends and
family. They stayed in the best hotels. Harry
made a list of where each princess was, so he
could keep track of them.

'Er . . . when is my first date?' Harry asked. He was already feeling nervous.

'Not till tomorrow,' said the queen. 'We need to tidy you up a bit first. The princesses won't be very impressed if you arrive looking like you usually do.'

The queen clicked her fingers . . .

. . . and suddenly Harry was surrounded by his own gaggle of stylists and hairdressers. They snipped and brushed and sprayed and styled and dressed him in the kind of clothes he hated. But his parents were pleased.

'Well I never!' said the king. 'You're actually quite good-looking.'

'He takes after me in that department,' said the queen. 'Come to think of it, he's got my brains too. Anyway, everything seems to be going to plan.'

But alas, the queen had spoken a little too soon.

Always Something Missing

Harry's first date was with Princess Miranda. She seemed nice enough, but she did spend most of the time looking at herself in her mirror. Harry also had to do most of the talking.

Harry asked her what kind of books she liked reading.

'Books?' she said, looking disgusted. 'Oh, I absolutely *hate* reading . . .'

'Well then, how did you get on?' said the queen later, after the date.

'Sorry, Mother,' said Harry. 'I'm afraid I've crossed her off my list.'

'Not to worry,' said the king. 'There are plenty more girls out there!'

Next up was Princess Gertrude, and she seemed more promising. She didn't keep looking at herself in her mirror, and she talked.

In fact she talked and talked and talked, and she was still talking when Harry finally ran away screaming.

'Don't tell me,' said the queen. 'You've crossed her off the list too.'

Harry shrugged and got ready for the next date. That was with Princess Scarlett.

She liked reading, but then they got on to the subject of computer games.

'Anyone who likes playing computer games must be a total idiot,' she said.

Harry rather enjoyed crossing her name off his list.

He crossed off two more in quick succession. Princess Clementine was horribly snooty, and Princess Grizelda turned out to be a lot scarier than she sounded on her profile . . .

The dates went on, and soon Harry began to feel really fed up. Oh, some of the princesses were lovely. Quite a few liked reading and riding and even computer games.

But none were right for him. There was always something missing.

'So is that it?' said the king, as Harry crossed the last name off his list. 'You're being far too fussy, Harry. We'll have to take another look at those websites.'

'No,' said the queen. 'I think it's time for Plan B.'

'Right, Plan B!' said the king. 'Remind me what that is again?'

The queen sighed. 'Sometimes I think I should have been a little more fussy myself . . .' she muttered. 'Plan B is a Grand Ball here at the palace, remember? We'll invite girls from all the noble families in the country.'

'Yes, of course!' said the king. 'That's bound to produce a result!'

Harry wasn't so sure. But he didn't say a word.

The Grand Ball

They started preparing for the Grand Ball the very next day. The palace was cleaned from top to bottom, the great hall was decorated and the best musicians were hired. Invitations were sent to every noble family in the country.

Amazing smells wafted in from the kitchen, but Harry wasn't allowed down there. The queen sent for the stylists and hairdressers again, and Harry spent hours being snipped and brushed and sprayed and dressed . . . in a totally new outfit.

'I hate it,' he muttered. 'I look like a badly wrapped Christmas present.'

It was the evening of the ball, and Harry was standing at the doors of the palace with his parents. The guests were starting to arrive in their coaches.

'It's better than mine,' said the king. 'I look like a badly stuffed sausage.'

'Just smile, will you?' the queen hissed. 'Welcome, good evening . . .'

Soon the great hall was packed, the band was playing and Harry could hardly hear himself think. He had to stand politely while an endless line of girls were introduced to him. One mother was particularly keen for him to meet both of her daughters.

After a while all the faces blurred into one, and Harry felt like he couldn't breathe. He had to get away and be on his own for a while.

34

'Just off to the bathroom!' he said to his parents. 'Back in a minute!'

But instead Harry ran to the quietest place in the palace – the library. He was sure nobody else would be there.

'Phew,' he said, as he closed the door firmly behind him.

'Oh, hello,' said a girl. She was startled and almost dropped the book she was holding. 'I probably should have asked before I came in, but I love libraries . . .'

'Really?' said Harry. He had been about to turn around and find another place to hide. But something about this girl made him want to stay.

'Do you read a lot?' he asked.

The girl sighed. 'Not as much as I'd like,' she said. 'What about you?'

'Oh yes, I'm always reading,' said Harry. 'Except when I'm doing other stuff. I like to go riding every day, and I love playing computer games as well.'

'Oh, wow. Those are the top two items on my list of Things I'd Like To Do.'

'Did you say . . . *list*?' murmured Harry.

His heart had just skipped a beat.

The Glass Slipper

Harry and the girl talked for ages. They soon discovered that they liked the same kind of books. They swapped loads of titles and the names of their favourite authors. But the thing that Harry kept coming back to was writing lists.

'Oh yes,' said the girl with a shy smile. 'That's definitely one of my quirks.

Before I go to bed I always write a list of the things I have to do the next day.'

'Me too!' said Harry, laughing.

'I couldn't live any other way.'

Suddenly the library clock started chiming. The girl looked at it – and went very pale.

'Oh no, it's nearly midnight!' she said. 'I have to leave!'

She dashed out of the library before Harry could say anything. He ran after her, but she pushed through the crowd in the great hall and fled from the palace.

He stood on the steps and watched as her coach drove off into the night.

Harry knew that she had taken his heart with her. But in exchange, she had left behind a beautiful, delicate glass slipper . . .

The next morning Harry's parents were cross with him.

'Where did you vanish to last night?' said the queen. 'You were supposed to choose one of those girls!'

'Well, I have,' said Harry. 'I met someone I really liked. But she ran off before I could find out her name or where she lives.'

'Oh, great,' said the king. 'He really does get his brains from you, dear.'

Luckily, Harry soon came up with a solution. He decided to tour the country with the glass slipper. They could get the girls who had been at the ball to try it on. And he would ask the girl it fitted to marry him . . .

It took a long time, and Harry saw a lot of feet. But he found the right girl at last.

Her name turned out to be Cinderella, and the wedding, of course, was wonderful. Everyone was pleased the story had a happy ending. 'It's just like a fairy tale,' they said.

'Right, that's it,' said the king. 'Here are the keys, Harry. We're off.'

'Hold on a second,' said the queen. 'Now are you two sure you've got everything under control? Is there anything we've forgotten to tell you?'

'Don't worry,' said Harry and Cinderella,
together. 'It's all written down.'

So Harry and Cinders went on making lists . . . happily ever after.